Yorkshi[illegible] Jokes

[illegible] Mitchell

Dalesman Books
in association with
Yorkshire Television
1989

The Dalesman Publishing Company Ltd.,
Clapham, Lancaster LA2 8EB.
First published (by Frank Graham) 1971
This edition 1987
Reprinted 1989

Drawings by Scott Dobson

ISBN: 0 85206 920 0

Uniform with this volume
"Teach Thissen Tyke" by Austin Mitchell

Printed in Great Britain by Peter Fretwell & Sons Ltd.,
Goulbourne Street, Keighley, West Yorkshire, BD21 1PZ.

INTRODUCTION
by Richard Whiteley

O'os Austin Mitchell any road?
I know 'oo e used ter be. That's enough.

Austin Mitchell war one 'ert' greatest of t'long line 'er Yorkshire nonentities: fowk sprung from t'sod o' God's Own Country oo tried ter make summat out o' nowt, but becum even bigger sods. 'Is name war up theer, inscribed among t'immortals in us Yorkshire Pantheon. It's written int'back lavatory behind t'stand i' Yorkshire County Cricket Club i' 'Eadingley wi't'names O' Sam Heginbotham, Enoch Greenwood, Albert Gaukroger an all t'others no one's ivver 'eard of since.

Awkward buggers all. An Austin war one o t'worst. Ee war a modest lad. Wi a lot ter be modest about. Ah can't write *Requiscat i' Yorkshire* on is grave — much as ah'd like — cos ah don't know weer it is. Or even if it is. Probably theer's some corner of a Lincolnshire field that is for ivver Yorkshire. So perhaps it's time to look back on his achievements. Not that that'll tek long, and say summat about im. Ee won't just a friend. Ee wa' more ner that. Eee owes me brass.

Is family cum fra 'Alifax. But Austin's mum won a competition in *t'Alifax Courier*. First prize war a week i'Hell, second two week i'Hull, third three week i'Alifax. She wunt' fourth and moved to Baildon for t'duration. So Austin wa' born i' a manger there. It's a funny thowt that both Yorkshire's best known has beens ('im and me) cum fra' t'same little Yorkshire village. I lived i'igh Baildon, weer all t'big knobs ang out. Austin lived i'low Baildon, weer t'outside nessies wor. But n'er mind that — a've allus looked up to im. (He'd be a six footer if he stood proper).

Ee went ter Woodbottom Council School. Like 'arold Wilson ee went ter school i'clogs. Probably t'same pair. Tha' knows what these Labour fowk are like. Then t'West Riding decided ter do summat ter improve education i'Baildon. They sent 'im ter Bingla. Int' sealed bus. Like Lenin.

Austin got educated cos 'ee didn't know that 'ee war going into telly. Ee got is C.O.D. at Shipley Post Office, 'is P45 at Shipley Labour, an' an Oxford Fellowship int' winter sales. Ee want allus int' telly. There war a time when ee used to work for a living. But then ee war lucky. Yorkshire Telly war that anxious for a feller wi' a Yorkshire accent they'd 'a tekken an Orang Outang wi' t'DTs if 'eed ad one. Austin as all t' reet qualifications. T'boss said 'e ad a reet good face fer telly — 625 lines — and ee got t'job.

Ee became right famous. Ee'ad "t'Immoff Syndrome". Fowk used to cum up to 'im int' street an say, "Ee, it's 'Immoff telly." Ee used ter go t't four corners o't civilised world: Middlesbrough, Barnoldswick, Sheffield an 'Ull to open bazaars, pubs, Galas, pubs, Sales of Work, pubs, and Fetes, some of 'em worse ner death. But ee war modest about fame. I remember going ont'train wi 'im to London. Austin war reading t'paper. T'chap opposite pulled it down and sez "Ah know thee. Tha's Austin Mitchell." "Hum," sez Austin and puts t'paper back up again. T'chap pulls it down. "Tha' war at Bingley Grammar School wi me." "Hum," sez Austin 'cos ee reckons not ter like beein' recognised. Ee puts t'paper back. "Ay cum on now," sez t'bloke, pulling it down agean, "Whats tha bin doin sin then?"

Ah remember when ee first went into politics. Ee went on 'is meat round wi' a yellow rosette to show 'is support for Gladstone. 'Til ee fund Home Rule weren't for Yorkshire. Then Ramsey MacDonald spoke to 'im at a seance. So ee joined t'Labour Party. Allus kind ter t'underdog, Our Austin. Then ee war a Yorkshire Nationalist and went round painting "Hs" off Steep ill signs as a protest. Finally at t'height of 'is fame ee took 'is 'ook. Vanished. There were them as said "Will ye no cum back agean." There war more as said "Good Shuttance." There war all kinds of rumours. Some said 'eed gone into politics. 'Is mother thinks ee's in prison. She's 'appier that way. Some said 'eed gone ter New Zealand. Some said eed got lost i' Lincolnshire an been 'etten. Some said eed gone ter worship at t'tomb of t'Unknown Elecution teacher 'i Grantham in 'opes of becoming Prime Minister. Some said ee war living i' poverty, others that 'eed gone mad and gone ter live in a padded cell i'Sowerby Brigg. No flowers bi request. An tha'd be daft as a besom brush ter send brass. Austin war a Yorksher Joke issen. Clogs ter crap i' wun generation. Ee allus wanted ter be t'first Prime Minister of Home Rule Yorkshire.

But I reckon ee waint cum back. It's 'is round i'pubs all ower t'county. As been for years. Ee's been forgotten — but not forgiven. Oo'iver's got 'im can keep 'im. Is jokes weren't funny. Ee wern't awther. As tha' can see by reading this. Nor is 'is introduction which ah rescued from 'is papers wi t'Official Receiver. 'Ahv'e cleaned off t'chip grease. 'Ere it is.

Richard Whiteley (Wi' tong in cheek).

Acshully, he were a grand lad. (Also wi' tong in cheek).

Yorkshire Humour

A thesis submitted for the PhD in Yorksher Studies, Barnsley College of Fish and Chip Knowledge.

It's difficult to write about Yorkshire humour. There isn't any. Southerners would say that this could be the briefest book since the *Norman Tebbit Charm Guide,* Neil Kinnock's *Chronicle of Life at Number 10* and David Owen's *Manual of Party Unity.* They think Yorkshire fowk have all the fun and gaiety of a week of wet Wednesdays int' dole queue i'Wandsworth. That's because Southerners don't laugh, they just giggle. They don't understand the north. They condescend to it. They don't have any humour. Just fashion. So they're not telling jokes to make people happy, they're showing off. Southerners have heads as empty as a Yorkshireman's pockets. So humour is fashion for them. Today's favourite fun is tomorrow's dead duck. There was satire ("You don't use new Wilson new Wilson uses you" — South: Roars and fits of giggles. North: Silence) Then came sick jokes: "Mummy, why can't I go swimming with the other boys?" "Cos your iron lung won't float." Then black humour, something to do with British Coal (Née NCB). Finally there's Mrs. Thatcher. Next week something else will tickle the fragile fancies of Finchley.

Humour's too serious for that. We're loyal to our jokes. They never change. Up here in the real world life's hard. So are we. There's no hiding from reality. Life's short. So there's no time to waste giggling around. Humour's basic. It deals with the eternal verities.

Some say that Yorkshire fowk are mean: like Aberdonians without the same generosity of spirit. Not true. I'll bet a half-penny that you can't find a mean Yorkshireman. What we are mean with is words. The air's cold. Tonsils freeze easily if mouths are open. We're a tribe. Tribes communicate by grunts and codes. They know each other too well for words. We're suspicious. Particularly so of those with too many words. That's a clear demonstration they've nothing to say. Our motto is:

Ear all see all say nowt
Ate all, sup all, pay nowt
An if tha ivver does owt for nowt
Do it for thissen.

So our general approach is

If tha knows nowt, say nowt
If tha knows summat, say nowt.

Someone with the gift of the gab must be trying to hide something behind all those unnecessary words:

Some tawk becos they think they're born
Wi'such a lot o'wit

Some seem to tawk to let fowk know
They're born wi'out a bit
Some tawk i'hopes 'as wot they say
May 'elp ther fellow men
But t'moast at tawk just tawk becoss
They like to 'ear thersen.

Life is hard in Yorkshire so we're more concerned with basic realities than any other part of the country. We face up to reality and make the best of it. Like this:

We're all dahn int' coil-oil
Weer t'muck slahts ont' winders
We've burnt all us coil
And we're agate burning t'cinders
When t'bumbailiffs come
They'll nivver find us
Cos we're all dahn in t'coil oil
Weer t'muck slahts ont' winders.

So most Yorkshire stories end happily in *Rigor Mortis*. Like that. Or like this:

Joah Jolly bowt a fahry 'oss
It cost him fifty pounds
One fine day ee went away
To 'ave an unt wi't'ounds
First fence Joah cum to
Ee sez "Nah Lad Goah"
Ee cleared that fence
Wi'out 'is 'oss
An' that were t'end on Joah.

It's Yorkshire that makes us Yorksha. We don't chuck owt around: money, words, jokes, laughs. Harry Secombe says a bloke in Bradford once told him after his act, "That war reet grand. Ah almost 'ad to laugh." The best way to appreciate these jokes is with a straight face and a look of misery. Then everyone will know you're enjoying it. Not that there is any alternative. Enjoyment is compulsory. These jokes are tried and tested. Through the ages they've been handed down from father to son. So we know them backwards. We love them too much to laugh at them. Or to say anything about them. Words have got to be treated economically too. Why waste them? You'll only have to think of more if you do. They might wear out and need replacing. Best remember the jokes, like we Yorkshiremen do, then repeat the numbers to every Yorkshireman you meet. You'll give a lot of quiet pleasure to a lot of Yorkshiremen. You may even reduce Southerners to hysterical giggles but you'll have to read the jokes out to them. With sub-titles. Unless you chew broken glass first.

In Yorkshire you've got to work hard and be a bit careful. We know what we like. We like what we know. Like these jokes. Fashion and repartee are irrelevant. Say you don't like someone with your hands rather than chilling your tonsils by opening your mouth. The only punch line you'll ever need is the one perfected by the Heckmondwike Postgraduate School of Wit, Repartee and ASDA Adverts:- "Get Knotted."

We keep our humour for the really important things in life. All true Yorkshire jokes (and all Yorkshire jokes are true, we're not an imaginative people who make things up like the Irish or the Welsh) are about the real essentials: death, disease, dialect, dog dirt and defeats at cricket. Since the Health Service there's been less of the first two which doesn't stop us thinking about either (or awther) when we're angry. There's certainly been too much of the last two. Yet we know that the divine order will re-assert itself. It's not for nothing that God is a Yorkshireman. Both defeats at cricket and dog dirt will eventually vanish from our lives. Meanwhile let's enjoy them, the jokes can be a bit of light relief. Note though, that while we are allowed to make jokes about ourselves we do so in the way a wine fanatic appreciates a fine wine. If you're not a Yorkshireman you're not allowed to repeat or even read any of these jokes. You must not smile. If you value your teeth.

The jokes have been carefully tested in workingmen's clubs throughout the county after being selected from samples submitted by a panel of such Con. Secs. and W.M.C. Committee Members as were out of prison at the time. They were then rated from five star to one on a complex grading system. The highest accolade is given to those jokes which produced no noise or giggles at all but heightened the naturally depressed expression on the faces of our test panel. The lowest ratings went to those which produced some form of reaction or the suspicion of a smile. Anything which produced more was immediately excluded from consideration and submitted to the Yuppie Joke Book shortly to be available under plain cover in Sloane

Square.

Let's start with the best and most basic Yorkshire joke in each category to display the rich diversity of Yorkshire humour:

Category One. Death

T'undertaker war int'parlour composing t'corpse an' removing t'smile so ee could meet is maker, t'great Tyke in t'sky. There's a knock at t'door. Ethel, t'widow, goes t'door. There's Fred's old mate Joe not knowing Fred's dead cos ee war tekken reet sudden.

"Ello Mrs., Fred in?" sez Joe.

"Nay. Ah'm sorry to ave t' tell thi. Fred's dead," she sez, all sobbing and bawling.

"Eee. Ah'm reet sorry to eer that," sez Joe, tekking is 'at off. "Did ee say owt about a pot o' paint?"

Category Two. Disease

Sam goes t'doctor. "Can tha give us summat ter mek us costive bound?" ee sez. "Ah've got awful diarrhoea."

"Sorry to hear that," sez t'doctor. "How long have you had it?"

"Ah don't reetly know," sez Sam. "Ah didn't find out till I took mi bicycle clips off."

Category Three. Dialect
Visitor arrives in Bradford. Wanting a local paper ee sez to t'lad, "I can't remember the one I enjoyed last time. But I know it started with a T."
"Tha' daft bugger," sez t'lad. "They all do. There's t'Telegraph, t'Argus and t'Observer."
Category Four. Dog Dirt
"Dad, sitha yon dog 'umping us Rover like ee war a wheelbarra'," sez t'little lad. 'Is Father belts im. To teach im some manners. "Ow many times 'ave I telt thee not ter say 'sitha'."
Category Five. Defeats at Cricket
Yorkshire are in difficulties at Bramhall Lane. The world's best bowlers can make no impression on Lancashire. The restive crowd shouts advice, "Put Fred on." After a time, "Put Ray on." Despairingly, "Put thissen on Close." Finally, and with more feeling, "Put t'clock on. Then we can all gerrome."

Now you are ready, dear reader (but not that dear given t'price o' t'book), to be made really miserable. Put the world's finest jokes into these five categories embracing the finest things of life. Grade them to taste. Now read on. It will make all those years at school seem worthwhile. Thanks for the brass.

Austin Mitchell
(Formerly Famous Person)

Now for us Jokes

Let's kick off with a rustic joke from the farming villages of the Dales and the East Riding. Here's a yarn from Wetwang, not very far from Driffield . . .

Sheila Todd cum back to t'village full of ersen after t'first term at York University. As she walked into the farmyard she saw her dad behind a wall wielding a pitch-fork.

"Hello daddy," she said, as though she had a mouthful of broken glass, "do tell me what you are doing."

Her dad's eyebrows raised a notch or two at his daughter's newly acquired accent.

"Muck-spreadin'," he grunted.

As soon as she got into the parlour young Sheila let fly at her mam.

"Really, mummy, I do think you ought to do something about father's language. Can't you ask him to refer to his present activity as 'manure-spreading'?"

"Nay, lass," said her mam. "It's tekken me twenty year to git him to call it muck."

Electricution teachers are allus trying to do that sort o' thing too. They want us to talk like we don't. Like the keen young teacher in Dore in Sheffield teaching her class the proper use of words. Which is something that's difficult to put over in Sheffield.

"Now class," she sez, "I'd like you to make a sentence using the word 'Charming'." The first girl to put her hand up said, "We went to the station and a young man held the door open for us and mummy said he was charming."

The next little boy hadn't said much since he'd arrived from Crooks the week before. Now he just said "Pregnant." "But, Arthur," said the teacher, "that's nothing to do with charming." "Yes it 'as, Miss. When us sister told me dad she war pregnant ee just said, 'Charming. Bloody charming'."

'Appen yer've not 'eard o't' Wombwell Birth and Burial Benefit Society. It 'as a motto ower t'door, "We Protect You from Womb to Tomb— Well." It does too. Thanks to the W.B.B.B.S., Wombwell produces the bonniest babies and the best burials in Yorkshire. Fowk come from miles around to see 'em. In fact ah mind t'time Jebb Yates's funeral were coming up t'ill from Darfield. There's these two miners off 'ome. Procession passes 'em wi' t'coffin and five 'undred mourners (Jebb war 92 so ee'd saved for a good benefit an' 'is widow 'ad a cartload o' green stamps). "Oo's funeral is it then?" sez one miner t'tother. "Dunno — must be 'im in t'box. 'Im 'at's driving looks all right," sez t'other. It war just at that moment, right on t'brow o' t'ill, that t'coffin rolled off t'hearse, crashed ont' t'ground, slid through t'mourners and past t'miners, lurching an' crashing an' rolling, top ower tip, getting faster and faster, until it crashed int' t'wall by t'shops at t'bottom o' t'ill. Owd Jebb 'adn't been a life long member of the W.B.B.B.S. for nowt (it war ten bob a year even int'owd days when Wombwell fowk war wiping t'sweat off their brow w't'slack o' their stumochs). Wi' great presence o' mind Jebb gets out o' t'shattered coffin, goes int' t'chemists and sez, "Ave yer got owt ter stop mi coffin?"

The Honorary Secretary and Treasurer of the Wombwell Birth and Burial Benefit Society is owd Enoch Dobson. Been doin' it all 'is life, an' full time since t'pit closed an' ee war declared recumbant. Ee's many a tale o't' burials they've paid for. And many a neet at t'Wombwell Labour Club ee 'as 'em killing thersels not laughing at t'comic ways some fowk 'as died.

There war t'time Enoch went round for Joe's subscription. Instead o' getting t'money ee finds Mrs. Joe a widow, waiting to collect t'benefit. "Ee ah'm sorry to 'ear Joe's passed on," Enoch sez, putting 'is collection book away.

"Can ah 'ave a last look at 'im? Ah've known 'im since we war lads tha knows."

"Ah know that lad. Come in," sez Widow Joe. There int' parlour Joe's laid out, ready for t'undertaker.

"Well ah'll be beggered," sez Enoch, "Ee does look well dunt ee."

"An' so ee should," sez Widow Joe, "we'd just come back from us 'olidays i' Brid."

Story Enoch likes telling best when ee's at t'club is t'time ee went round to Stubleys oo war months behind wi' t'dues. Ee knocks ont'door thinking they won't come like last time. But it opens an Lillian Stubley comes to t'door wiping 'er 'ands on 'er apron.

"Afternoon Mrs.," sez Enoch, "ahv'e come for t'dues. Bert in?"

"Nay, ee's just killed hissen. Ee went down t' t'allotment to cut a cabbage an' ee'd 'ad a few jars, tripped ower t'marrow, fell ont'knife and killed hissen. Just like that."

"Ee ah'm reet sorry to hear that Mrs.," sez Enoch, who knows what's to be done in these cases. "What did yer do?"

"Only thing we could do. We 'ad to open a tin o'peas."

Fowk dies from all sorts o' things i'Wombwell. Miners die from Telephononewmeaoconiusis, some 'ave even been known to die from Boredom, 'an Enoch once 'ad a bloke as died o' drink. Ee worked int'Brewery in Barnsley. Yer know t'one. Its got posters all ower t'place. When she cum Maggie Thatcher thowt t'posters war saying what Barnsley thought o't' 1987 election result. Roy Mason 'ad to explain to 'er what "Barnsley Bitter" wor all about cos Mag's a secret shandy lass. Anyroad this bloke worked in't brewery for years until t'day ee fell int' t'vat an' drowned. They phoned Enoch an' asked 'im to break news t't'widow. They felt they'd better do it that way cos Enoch's tactful an' ee knows about these things. Once before when someone 'ad drowned they'd sent t'bloke's mate round to break it. Eed just gone up t't' door, knocked and when t'Mrs. came eed said, "Are you t'widow Walker?"

"Ah'm nowt o't'sort," she said, "ah'm married to Jack Walker."

"Tha's not," t'mate replied, "tha's t'widow Walker. Ees drowned."

Enoch knows 'ow to do it better na this. Ee knows we've all got to cock us clogs sometime. When ee tells 'em t'widows don't feel so bad about it. So this time ee goes t't'ouse, just knocks on t'door and tells 'er straight away.

"Ah'm reet sorry to 'ave to tell yer, Mrs., but yer husband's drowned to deearth i't'beer vat at work."

"Ee that's orful," she sez, "Cans't tell me one thing. Did ee suffer much?"

"Nay, ah doant reckon so," Enoch sez, "they tell me ee 'ad to get out three times to go t't' lav."

Still that's enough about fowk deeing. Tha'll think we talk about nowt else in Yorkshire, an' if tha wants to get more stories about it tha can allus go an' see Enoch. Ee's int' Wombwell Labour Club most neets. If tha' buys 'im a pint ee'll tell thi that many stories about dead fowk, ee'll kill yer.

Then there was the political meeting on behalf of the Labour candidate in true blue Harrogate.

Candidate:	If you good people vote for us we will bring down Income Tax.
Voice from back:	What about Old Age Pensions?
Candidate:	If you good people vote for us we will increase Old Age Pensions.
Voice from back:	What about prostitutes on our streets?
Candidate:	If you good people vote for us we will drive Prostitution underground.
Voice from back:	I thought so. Ruddy Labour's pampering the miners again.

If there's one thing we take more serious than us jokes i' Yorkshire it's us sport. None of this gentleman amateur tradition. We play nowt for fun and there's some of us that good they play nowt for nowt. We play to win an' if we can't win we're not going to play. Which is why we've not done much about ping pong. We usually win t'cricket, t'soccer an' t'rugby, so we've to leave summat to t'others.

Becoss we usually win we can relax t'pressure from time ter time an' 'ave a laugh. Yer'll get plenty from Bradford Park Avenue one o't' few Yorkshire teams that never wins nowt so as to console fowk outside t'county if Leeds and Sheffield an' Hull wins everything else. Ah used to watch Park Avenue when ah war a kid, back in them days when Bradford Co-op used to pay a divi. Ah war thinking o'mi last visit to Park Avenue t'other week as ah went past t'ground. Last time ah went were t'last time Park Avenue scored a goal. It came up on "All Our Yesterdays" only last week. These days t'team teks a lap of honour if they get a corner.

One ot' sports reporters for t'*Yorkshire Sports* wor telling me as we did our arm bending exercises int'Alex t'other neet that Halifax Town's manager rang up Don Revie for a spot of advice on how to get Halifax Town int' t'First Division like grown up clubs (to be fair ee did say they wouldn't mind coming a bit below Liverpool — but only a little bit mind). Mi mate said t'telephone call went summat like this —

Don Revie: "Allo".

Halifax Acting Manager, Captain, Groundsman and Bottle Washer: 'Alifax Town 'ere Don. Can yer give us some 'ints about 'ow your lads train to get so good?"

Don Revie: "Happy to help lad. We need some competition. We lay out eleven dustbins in a team formation and each player dribbles the ball round them and tries to dazzle them with science. It improves ball control no end."

H.A.M.C.G.A.B.W.: "Thanks a million Don. We'll try it. Remember me to Football."

Nice bloke Don Revie. A couple o' days later ees back ont'phone to 'Alifax, anxious to find out how they'd got on.

Don Revie: "Allo. Don Revie here."

H.A.M.C.G.A.B.W.: "Allo Don. 'Alifax Town 'ere."

Don Revie: "Well how did you get on with my new method of training?"

H.A.M.C.G.A.B.W.: "Bloody awful. T'dustbins won 2-1."

Ah thowt ah might go an' see a match at 'Alifax Town t'other week. Just for old times' sake. Ah rang t'ground an' a bloke as called issen "Mr. Mayor" answered.
"What time's t'kick off," ah sez. "What time can yer get 'ere," sez t'voice at t'other end. Fact when ah did get there ah 'ad to shake 'ands wit'team an' there war no one else theer apart from some bloke on't kop writing a poem. It went summat like "I wandered lonely as a cloud . . ." but ah can't remember t'rest. Ee did tell me but ah'm not sure ow much is word's worth.

Any road it's lonely ont'terraces in 'Alifax. If yer want a crowd yer've to go to Elland Road. They get thousands there an' some on 'em come through t'turnstile. In fact one neet when Leeds war playing Frank Varos an' 'is team t'ground war that crowded that a bloke from Menston oo'd just managed to shove 'is way in war knocked unconsumate by t'crowd pouring int't'ground. Ee war left hanging there ower t'barrier. When ee cum too t'groundsman war sweeping up an' there weren't another soul around. Neither on 'em war best pleased.

"Gerrout," sez t'groundsman, thinking from t'look on 'im that ees dealing wi'a bloke fra Unslet. "They've all gone 'ome."

"Eck," sez t'bloke, realising ees missed t'game. "What war t'score then?"

"It war a draw — nil nil."

"Eee war it? Well what war t'alf time score?"

Still we take us football less seriously than cricket, because that's one of t'great religious denominations in Yorkshire. There's Protestants who don't agree wi't'umpire's verdict, Roamin Catapults who go t't'matches outside county an' those who're drunk incapable at any one time. In fact in t'old days Yorkshire versus Lancashire matches war like an action replay o't'Wars o't'Roses int' fifteenth century. In fact at one match at Headingley there war this bloke there sticking his fillings in an keepin up a running commentary on t'match like —

"What's tha think tha's batting wi — a closet seat?"

"Weer's tha white stick umpire?"

"My brother's got more life in 'im an' ees on t'sick."

"Kill t'umpire." "Kill t'batsman." "Kill t'bowler."

In fact ee war for killing that many folk there war some as thowt ee were an undertaker fra' Otley on a slack week. It went on for so long they 'ad to send a committee member down fra't'pavilion to 'ave a word wi'im.

"Are you fra Yorksher," sez t'committee member. "Nay," said t'bloke." "Well, are yer fra' Lancashire." "Nay," sez t'bloke, wi't mouth like a parish oven.

"Well then," sez t'committee man, "tha mun mind thi own bloody business."

It's not all enmity though. Ah've known some right grand fowk fra' Lancashire. Course they all live ower 'ere now, but they war grand fowk afore they came. Mi cousin Stan lives up at Heptonstall. Toffee nosed lot there. Ee right looks down on fowk fro Hebden Bridge an even, on a clear day, on fowk fra Lancashire. Well, Stan went ower to Old Trafford for a Yorkshire versus Lancashire match last year an' ee's sitting there an suddenly realises summat. "Damn it," ee sez in a loud voice. "Ah've left mi jock i'Ebden Bridge." There's silence all round while fowk tries to translate what he's just said. Then one unusually quick witted Lancastrian works it out. "Never mind lad," says the kindly Lancastrian. "My wife'll give you some lunch if you pop home during the break" (speaking slowly like they do when talking to someone who's ten-pence to 't shilling). "Just go through yon gate, turn left around the back then turn right and there's No. 23 Red Rose Row. My wife'll cook lunch for you." Stan'll never refuse owt free even if it were leprosy in Bradford (it used to be amazing what you could get at Taylor and Parsons) so off he trots. Two hours later Stan gets back, brussen, but all red faced and flustered. Ee comes dashing up to his new Lancashire pal. "Ah've got some real bad news for thee I'm afraid lad. Thi 'ouse burnt down an' thi wife's been carted away to Hospital." "I've some worse news for thee," says t'Lancastrian. "Boycott's out."

Those were the days when yer used to get crowds at county matches. Now the only cricket event that brings t'crowds pouring in is Yorkshire County Cricket Club meetings. Some fowk say they're better entertainment than t'game itself these days. Fact ah've even 'eard they're trying to get Gillette to sponsor one every weekend an' committee members who lose their seats'll be executed. Good mornings begin with Gillettine. Still, there's a mate o'mine, Dirty Dick they call him, on account of the fact that ee war brought up in Barnsley. After t'last Yorkshire County Meeting ee war walking down t'steps o' Leeds Town Hall behind Brian Sellers an' another committee member. They're just about to cross t'road when a car comes roaring up an' misses them by a flicker of a vicar's knickers as they both leap back on't'pavement. "Hell's bells," sez t'committee member to Brian Sellers, "that war Close."

Funny really. There's not only t'crowds gone from cricket but even t'daft things fowk used to say. In fact there war so much wit at Yorkshire County Matches that they could make t'comic at Keighley Workingmen's Club look gormless. Like when Fred Trueman war bowling agin Lancashire wi' an umpire ut came fra Rochdale an' were determined Lancashire war going to win — nay that's impossible, ah mun mean not loss too badly. Fred bowls. Wham an' it 'its 'is pad stuck right in front o't middle stump. "Owzat", yells Fred, an' 'alf the team wi 'im. "Not out," says t'umpire. Next ball from Fred comes down. Wham. It 'its t'bat and just whizzes past bail. T'bail shakes but dunt fall off. "Owzat," yells Fred. "Not out," says t'umpire, a bit annoyed like. Fred teks 'is run again. Whizz. Wham. Crash, an' t'middle stump goes flying, sails twenty yards in t'air and crashes down, shattered. "By 'ell," says Fred, "ah nearly 'ad 'im then."

That reminds me of another of Fred's cracks. Ee war in a Gentlemen versus Players game one time when they'd really dredged round and got some real gentlemen, so refeened, ee got 'is finger stuck up 'is nostril when ee war drinking tea and war incapacitated for t'rest o't'game. Well there's one of these gentlemen coming out to face Fred's bowling. Strides out to the crease in leisurely fashion. Surveys the field slowly as if smelling each fielder under t'armpits, teks ten minutes getting 'is centre, gets sight screen shifted and then 'as to adjust 'is gloves. "Ready now," ee finally calls. My cousin Stan oo war there sez Fred came pounding down like a bankrupt stock Rolls run out of M.1 at Leeds. Crack. Ee's bowled first ball. "Very good ball my man," ee calls to Fred on 'is way back t't' pavilion. Fred spits on 'is 'ands. "Aye but it war wasted on thee."

Meanwhile at the Middlesbrough Metal and Related Trades Social Club . . . The Con. Sec. war furious. The club war chokka. Every man Jack on 'em war calling twenty t't'dozen. He couldn't start the Bingo.

Gracefully he rose in his podium, having the good sense to sway backwards and forwards instead of left to right. "Giuzbestovorder," he bawled, banging his hammer down. Some bothered to look up. Row went on.

The third minute he rose again, bellowing out with lungs of leather, "Giuzthebestovorder Pleez." Not a blind bit of notice.

He hadn't been Con. Sec. for fifteen years for nothing. He played his trump card. "Alreight," he announced in cold, measured tones, "if tha dunt all belt up this minute ah'll fetch t'comedian back on."

You could have heard a pin drop as Maisie called "Legs Eleven."

In the clubs of South Yorkshire the lads are even more difficult to please. At t'Royston Working Men's t'comic told t'Con. Sec., "I'm not going in there again unless we get a bit more attention." "Ah understand 'ow tha feels," sez t'Con Sec. "Gerrout."

This inscription is on the back of the door of the star dressing room at Fryston Miners' Welfare:

> "Remember all ye who sit here before venturing forth to entertain the patrons of this club.
>
> Jesus Christ the one and only Son of God was booked in here for a week one Easter.
>
> He did this truly amazing act of being crucified by sundry selected members of the audience, was certified dead by the Con. Sec. and was buried in the cellar under a barrel of mild.
>
> Three minutes later he rose again and was back on stage.
>
> The Con. Sec. paid him off with the words, 'Don't worry thissen lad. Tha might be an hit down South'."

Then there was the music teacher from Castleford who called his dog Grieg. When asked why, he said: "Because ee's allus wantin' to pee a'gint suite."

Some fowk reckon we're a bit rude i'Yorkshire. A good thump on't lug'ole'll soon teach em better. We speak as we find and if we don't like what we find then you can hardly blame us for pointing it out. Someone has to do it. Like mi mate Joss frae Thurgoland. Ee went down to London on a cheap weekend an' found that ee could pass time an' see London for practically nowt by going round an' round in t'underground ont'circle line. Ee war t'only bloke int' carriage when an ugly Southerner got on. Not just ugly. This bloke were like t'back end of a tram smash an' then some. Joss sat and stared at 'im, summat they don't seem to do int'south where they all look off in terror if yer so much as glance at em. Eventually t'Southerner siz, "Just what are you staring at my good man?"

Jos leans back. "Ah'm just thinking that tha's t'ugliest begger ah've ever seen."

Poor Southern lad sez, all upset like, "Well I can't help it, can I?"

"No," sez Joss, "but tha could 'ave stayed at 'ome."

Joss war nowt if not direct. Ah mind t'time ee went into Penistone to catch t'bus to Barnsley for t'market. It's Joss's turn to get on when t'conductor puts his arm across an' pushes Joss off again. "Gerroff," sez t'conductor, "we're full. Tha'll 'ave to wait for t'next."

"Oh aye," sez Joss, "an' 'ow long'll that be."

Conductor thinks ee's a right wit. "About thirty feet, like this un."

"Oh aye," sez Joss, "an' will it 'ave a closet ont'back wi a turd in like this un?"

Meanwhile back at the Copper Beech in Baildon the Con. Sec. was getting a bit aireated. On the stage Miss Doreen Golightly, singing for the price of her drinks, but makkin 'eavy weather of "Velia oh Velia The Witch of the Wood." The audience was chuntering on, knocking back its ale, crunching its chips, crumpling its bags and making like a civic banquet going down Browgate at fifty miles an hour. Doreen's dulcet tones were drowned.

The Con. Sec. plugged 'is mike into the Amp. Just as Doreen's 'itting 'er top note the room rang with the Con. Sec's command. "Shut up the lot o'yer. Give t'poor Cow a chance."

All told it's not really rudeness. We just see fowk for what they are. If they don't like it it's not our fault. There war this farmer out at Kilnsey. Small farm an' only father an' son to run it so there's not much to talk about. Father's dipping 'is sheep when t'neighbour's Land Rover roars int't'yard an' out gets Harris, red faced with anger, shouting, "Do you know what that lad o' thine 'as gone an' done now. Ee's made our Mary pregnant, that's what ee's done. Ah'll have 'is guts for garters when I get me 'ands on 'im."

"Eee ee's a dozy beggar," sez t'father. "Ee went an' broke a shovel last week."

At least that reaction's better than the Grandad to be might get further north. When a Bilsdale farmer with exactly the same complaint dashed into Farmer Blaydon's it was the wife who came to the door. "Made her pregnant 'as ee," she said thoughtfully. "Well, you'll have to wait till my husband comes home. I know he charges ten bob for the boar and £5 for the stallion, but I don't know how much ee charges for oor Willie."

Ah wan't there missen. When it 'appened ah wor down at t'Sun Inn i' Shipley. Me dad cum in wi'is little Yorkshire terrier, that hairy yer can't tell whether it's coming or going. There's this posh bloke at the bar and the Yorkie walks straight up to him and cocks his leg up against 'is Ush Puppies. Bloke didn't say a word. In fact ee war that nice about it ee took three crisps out of 'is bag and threw 'em on't floor for t'dog. Mi dad war dead relieved. "That's very nice of you," he sez, "t'dog wets thi trousers and tha gives 'im a crisp."

"Aye," said the bloke, "an' when I see which end picks t'crisp up I'll stick me boot int't'other."

And if your new suit doesn't impress your pals 'appen there are other ways to make them sit up . . .

John Thistlethwaite was allus bragging to his mates in t'Dolphin at Wakefield. This night he's cracking on that he knows every person in the world.

"Aw shaddup Cleverclogs. Tha's takin' thro' thi hat," said his mates, especially Kit.

Well this makes John fair nowty.

"Reet," he says, "come wi me."

Off they go, John and kit, to Buckingham Palace. Out into the grounds comes the Queen, sees John, waves to him and comes over and has a chat.

Still Kit didn't believe him.

Off they go to America to the White House, out comes President Reagan, and takes John inside for cocktails.

Still Kit didn't believe him.

So off they go to Europe and John introduces Kit to Kings, counts, dukes, Common Market ministers, peasants, priests, gigolos, Alpine guides, the lot. Finally they end up at the Vatican in Rome.

"Hang on a tick Kit. Ah'm just going up to see me mate the Pope."

Kit watches with thousands as the Pope comes out onto the balcony followed a second later by John.

Suddenly a little Italian fellow turns round to Kit and says, "Scuse, but oo ees dat fellow up there with John?"

They're not like us down South. Yer can live next to fowk down there for years and never speak to 'em. Not that they'd 'ave owt worth saying if yer did. They may 'ave all t'brass these days but they're still comics. Best ignored. Like the two Wharfedale farmers gone down to London during t'war to get away from t'urley of Burley. As they were strolling down Regent Street, gawping like hob-gobs, air-raid sirens went and everyone ran for shelters and tube stations except our two Tykes. A.R.P. man came hurtling up to them on a bike shouting, "Take Cover. Take Cover", but farmer Coverdale tells im "Geronwiyer. It dunt apply to us. We doant live i'London."

Still we do get down South from time to time, to go down to collect cups and such like for t'Soccer League ant'Rugby League. Ah mind t'time a bus load o' lads fra Castleford went down to watch Cass win t'cup. Coach is finding its way back to Wallace Arnold land along Oxford Street when one ot'lads looks out an' yells, "Sitha there's Seth Newman." Right as rain, there's old Seth, drunk as a posser 'ead staggering along. They stop t'coach, grab Seth, an' after a long struggle drag 'im back int't Sharrah.

Off they go back ter civilisation. Three in the morning they're back at Castleford hammering away at Seth's door. No answer. For a quarter of an hour, no answer. Suddenly next door's bedroom window shoots up. "Quiet yer noise," yells t'next door neighbour. "It's no use 'ammering for Seth at this time o'neet. Ee's gone down ter London for t'week."

Even outside London it's sometimes difficult to get yourself understood. Jack Higgins took a week off from Kellingley Main to go to Wales and couldn't understand a word they said. In t'boozer they all spoke Welsh. Outside no one spoke at all. Dead miserable ee was, until after four days he found someone to teach him Welsh. That night he recited his Welsh phrases over an over in bed. Next morning up early to try them out but there's not a soul around. Even in the country round about: not a soul. About to give up an' go back to bed, his spirits soar when ee sees a lonely figure on a bike pedalling towards him. As the figure drew nearer Jack leapt into the road shouting. "Jacky Da. Jacky Da." The cyclist kicked 'im out of the road an' grunted, "Get out ot'road yer dozy Welsh bastard."

An Ingelborough farmer's on the bus back home from Skipton. Sitting next to him a chatty American tourist doing the Dales. She chatters on trying to get the taciturn farmer talking.

"Say, did you have a good day at Market today?"

"Appen."

"I think Skipton's a beautiful place. Don't you agree?"

"Appen."

"This surely must be one of the most beautiful parts of Yorkshire."

"Appen."

Desperately she turned her attention to the dog.

"What a beautiful dog. Have you had him long?"

"Appen."

"And what's the little fellow's name?"

"Roger Bacon."

At last she saw a chink in the conversational armour. She forged in. "What an unusual name for a dog. Why on earth do you call him Roger Bacon?"

"Because o' what ee does ter t'pigs."

Don't think that no Southerners ever come North. A lot come to Wakefield. It's one ot'best jails int'country. Jaspar St. John-Fotheringay-Smyth came up for twenty years for confidence tricks. Looking round 'is cell the first day ee wondered 'ow ee'd pass the time cos it wer bigger than 'is flat in London an' more room than ee war used to. Then ee spotted a couple o' fleas ont' mattress (last man in war also from t'south). Ee thinks "I'll train these little blighters. Wonderful way of passing the time and I'll make my fortune when I get out. Marvellous idea." For twenty year ee trained 'is fleas. They could

do all sorts o' fantastic tricks when ee war released. First thing ee does is go into the Dolphin for a pint. But ee can't wait to show 'is wonderful fleas. Ee gets out 'is matchbox puts em ont'counter an' siz t't'barman, "Tell me potman. Have you ever seen anything like this before?" Bartender crashes 'is 'and down ont'fleas, saying, "Aye, we get too many o' them things 'ere."

But then they are a bit taciturn like that in the Dales. In Pateley Bridge there were two farm hands in the road just outside the vicarage, fratching bitterly about what looked to me to be a dead horse. "It's a donkey." "Is it eck it's a mule." "Ah tell thi it's a donkey." "Tha needs thi 'ead looking at. It's a mule."

So it went on until the Rev. Fawthrop was drawn out by the noise. Being man of the cloth he quickly calmed them down. "It's an ass. It's the same animal that carried our Lord into Jerusalem. We must bury it with all due respect."

Reluctantly they agreed and began digging. Major Bagshaw appeared round the corner. Once a solider always a soldier. He called out, "What's that you're digging men? A fox hole?"

"Not according t't'Vicar."

Then there was the two fellows who met in a pub in Hull, where you see many strange sights in the boozers — everything from monkeys to man-eating mosquitoes. An' yer can nivver be sure whether fowk are swearing fit to bust or talking Swedish.

One fellow had a brown dog and the other a black one. As their owners argued who's was the fiercest the dogs flexed their muscles and bared their teeth. Very soon the two fellows were at each other's throats.

"My dog could murder yours," said the brown dog's master.

"My dog could crucify yours," said the black dog's master.

"Oh shut up will yer," said the landlord. "Ah've got a dog behind here will lick both those things at t'same time."

The match was agreed. Side-bets were laid. One fellow gave his dog a whisky, the other slipped his a sherry with an egg whisked up in it. Then the landlord produced his dog. It was spotted and had very short legs.

Slowly it lurched over to the brown dog and ate it. Then it did the same with the black dog.

As the dog belched the owners of the erstwhile dogs cried our aghast:

"Ere, what kind o' dog is that?"

"Well," replied the landlord, "afore I lopped its tail off and painted the spots on it, it were a crocodile."

Then there were the two old Dalesmen who lived in two old dilapidated cottages in Wensleydale. They were leaning on the garden wall talking to each other.

"Nar then Joe, 'ave just 'ad a letter from council, they're moving me into a new council flat next week."

"That's great," his friend says, "but what are you going to do with your pig?"

"Well, I'm taking him with me," he replied.

"But where are you going to put him?" Joe asks.

"I'm going to put it in the bedroom!"

"But what about the smell?" Joe asks.

"Chuff smell, pig'll soon get used to it."

Another pig joke . . . .

After spending weeks fattening up his pigs Fred Pickles drove them all down to Pickering market to sell them off.

In the pub he met Tom Dobbin who said he fancied buying a few pigs.

The two men were fairly good acquaintances and Fred wanted a quick sale so a bargain was struck. Fred let Tom have the pigs at a very reasonable price.

"Ah'll send thi a cheque in t'post," said Tom. They had a few bevvies to seal the deal.

Well, two weeks later Fred still hadn't heard a dickybird's from Tom. So he sent him a letter saying he'd appreciate the money.

He got a letter saying Tom would pay him next week. This went on for weeks until the two men met in the pub on market day again.

"Bah lad," muttered Fred, "tha's fed me reet up. If ah'd ha' known tha was nivver goin' ti pay, ah'd ha' charged thi twice as much."

Relations with Lancashire have never been good. It's partly because although they're no good at cricket they do make some effort at soccer and rugby league. But it's mainly because we're different sort o' fowk. Yorkshire's all hills an' moors. Lancashire's all mills an' . . . well perhaps not all. But there's always been a lot o' fratching. It began wi't'Wars ot'Roses. Red versus white. When ah went to school t'West Riding used to have t'white rose carved ont'desk seats so ah feel deeply about t'white rose. An' it's no wonder t'white rose won. Ah found this account of a Yorkshire victory in General Trumpington-Blatherskite's *Short History of Yorkshire Victories* (14 volumes). Evidently the Earl of Derby was marching over the Pennines with a huge Lancashire army when they spot a Yorkshireman on Studley Pike shouting "One Yorkshireman can beat fifty on yer." Just to make sure they send 100 Lancashire soldiers after him. None came back.

Next day there he was shouting "One Yorkshireman can beat 100 on yer." This time they send 200.

This went on for three days until one morning one battered bloodstained Lancashire soldier staggered into the Red Rose camp. "Let's get back home," ee gasped. "It's a trap. There's two of 'em."

It was two in the morning and a lamp flickered in an upstairs window of the tiny farm in Rosedale.

For Bill and Babs Bugby it was a great moment. Bill was holding the lamp as Doctor Foster was preparing to deliver his first-born.

Suddenly the Doctor held up a baby boy and Bill leaned nearer with the lamp to have a look.

"Ho'd on," said the Doctor, "there's another one comin'." Then he held up a baby girl.

"Twins," gasped Bill as he held the lamp nearer to have a look.

"Ho'd on," cried the Doctor, as out popped another baby boy.

Suddenly the room was pitched into darkness and Bill's boots clattered off down the stairs.

"Bring back that lamp," yelled the Doctor.

"No fear," shouted back Bill from the parlour. "Tha'll 'ave to manage baht it — t'dammed leet's attractin' t'little beggars."

Ah reckon we're t'best county because Yorkshire breeds 'em tough. Sometimes too tough. Ron Walker from Hunslet was a real tough nut. Ee'd thump yer soon as look at yer. Down at t'magistrates court ee 'ad a season ticket. Always in there. Until one day ee faced a more serious charge. The big league. This time a judge and jury. "Prisoner at the bar," yells the Clerk of the Court, "do you wish to challenge any member of the Jury." Ron looks 'em ower, "Well, ah'm not i' training, but ah'll try a couple o' rounds wit'fat one int' corner."

Yer can scratch even the poshest Yorkshireman and you'll find pure Tyke close to the surface. Take Joe Clogroyd. Been a miner at Waterloo Main for thirty years before it closed. Then ee struck lucky on the pools an' copped £100,000. Leaves 'is back to back. Sells 'is whippet. Ups to live round Whitby. An' being a sporting kind o' lad ee joins the Zetland Unt, or Hunt as they call it up there. Joe cut a marvellous figure on 'is new 'orse. Great chase they had. Joe was in on the death. Next day the Hunt Master comes round to Joe's new palace. "Look Mister Clogroyd," sez ee, "this is rather embarrassing and I don't want you to take it at all personal. But it is customary for riders to hounds to call 'Tallo Ho' rather than 'After the Bushy Tailed Swine'."

Still at least we've not as much to learn as they 'ave in some parts. Ah mind the Todmorden tackler oo left t'town just before t'first World War wi Bill Holt. Bill went to Germany. 'Is mate Tom went to Paris. Tom got back first. A tackler's a prince among weavers any road but now they clustered round wi'awe. "Is it like they say it is i'Paris," they said. "Well, ah can't say much," ee sez with the dignity tacklers 'ave. "But ah'll tell thi this. Sexual Intercourse is in its infancy i' Todmorden."

Course these days you don't have to go as far for that kind of experience. There's no mines left in Barnsley, but there's a hell of a lot of miners an ah met one int'White Art oo told me about 'is mate Jack Obbs as went down to London to see life. Ee goes along to t'Park Lane Ilton ter clock in an' when they ask 'im ter sign t'register ee makes 'is cross. Just then there's a gorgeous blonde walks past an' Jack sez t't'page, "Bloody Ummer, I could do wi a bit o' that." Page sez, "Well I think it might be possible to arrange a rendezvous for Sir, on the side you understand."

"Well gerron wi' it then," sez Jack, grabbing hold of t'register an' putting a ring round 'is cross.

"Pardon me, but why has Sir just done that," sez t'page.

"Tha dunt think as ah'm goin' ter go traipsing eround wi' yon blonde bit under mi own name does tha?"

Overheard in Heppy's Fish Restzurant in Wakefield:

"Ah wor reet sorry ah couldn't get to Bob's Bachelor Party last week. Wor it a good do?"

"Wor it eck. Everyone theer wor able to go to work t'next day."

There's these two old birds sitting int'Tennyson Bingo i' Bratford — that one 'ats named after t'best caller Bratford ever 'ad — an' there's a funeral procession goes past outside. One old bird begins to snuffle and sniffle that much she misses two calls. "Nay what's up wi' thi," says t'other. "Eee," she sez, "ah'm upset. Ee wor a good husband to me."

Yorkshiremen make admirable business men. Probably because they get their priorities right . . . .

There was this chap took a pub in a tiny village near Grassington. As soon as he opened the doors on his first day, in staggered an old yokel who could not have been a day under eighty. He glowered at the landlord, spat on the fire, hobbled to a seat in the corner and began bashing on the floor with his stick. This got the new landlord's back up, no mistake.

"What's ta want?" he asked.

"Look," said the old chap, "my name's Ned. Ah'm t'owdest in t'village and when I come in I allus sit 'ere. And when I bangs me stick I want a gill o'mixed reet sharp. So think on."

Gritting his teeth the new landlord served him. Then just as he was about to give old Ned a mouthful into the pub marched the local squire.

"Good day my man," said the squire. "I'll have six bottles of gin, eight bottles of Scotch, a dozen of sherry and a dozen of port. Oh, yes, and six crates of Tetley's Pale Ale and six of Guinness. Get your cellarman to put them in my landrover, and won't you join me in a large Scotch!"

As the Squire and the new landlord supped up old Ned began banging like fury with his stick. The Squire paid up and left. With his neck beetroot the landlord pulled a half and prepared to slam it down before old Ned. As he approached old Ned looked up: "Look lad. I'll gie thi a bit of advice. Thee look after thi regulars — yon beggar only comes in once a week."

In Cleckheaton there's not much to do except watch t'grass grow, so they live to a ripe old age. But none older than Josiah Igginbotham, t'owdest inhabitant at 95. T'Round Table got together an Clough of Cleckheaton proposed that they should do summat special to commemorate Josiah's 95th birthday. Since ee'd never been out of Cleckheaton in 'is life they decided to club together and send 'im to London for a couple o' days. New suit, new suitcase, new 'aircut an' off ee went. Two days later ee war back. Unimpressed. "Wor war it like?" they asked.

"Well, ah'll tell thi this. Cleckheaton's better na London." Ee war so contented that ee reached 105. This time t'Round Tablers as an even bigger whip round t'table an' sent 'im to Paris for a week. Same thing 'appened. "Cleckheaton's better na Paris," ee declared.

They didn't need to spend any more money sending 'im ter Sheffield for t'day. Ee died at 109. Ee passed ower to'other side. An' this time ee 'ad to admit it. 'Is eyes opened wide. 'Is mind marvelled. Soon ee couldn't contain 'is wonder. "Ah've got ti admit it," ee yelled. "'Eaven's better na Cleckheaton." Just then up came a man wi' a long tail and a pitchfork an' sez, "Shut up you old fool. This isn't heaven."

Arthur an' Ted are sitting 'aving a quiet pint in' Victory Club i' Stocksbridge. They've just read t'*Sun* so they're talking about Permissive Society an' 'ow much it cost to join. "Yer know old mate," sez Arthur, "ah nivver 'ad any sexual relations wi't wife before ah married er . . . Did you?" "Dunno," sez Ted, "wot war 'er maiden name?"

Yorksher's a language all on its own. When t'Yorkshiremen on t'test team (that's nearly all o't'team) didn't want to be overheard all they 'ad to do war to talk i' Yorksher. So there's a lot o' jokes none from South o' Doncaster can understand. Like the bloke from Oxford who was asking the class at St. Helen's County Primary in Monk Bretton where they were going for their holidays. Course they all were going to Bridlington. Except one lad oo pipes up, "Mi dad's tekkin' us t't'lakes i' Barnsley." "Then he's pulling your leg sonny, there's no lakes in Barnsley." Little lad dun agree. "Well mi dad sez there's more lakes na works i'Barnsley."

Or take the little Bingley lad sitting on Ireland Bridge bawling 'is 'ead off. A well to do looking bloke rushes out of the antique shop to ask 'im what's up.

"Me mate's fell int'watter."

Without further ado the bloke strips off 'is Brown and Muffs suit, jumps ower t'bridge, dives in every pool, wades all round, comes out ten minutes later dripping. "Sorry, son," pant, pant. "I can't find him. Will it help you to tell me how it happened?"

The lad stops bawling long enough to say, "Well, ah just opened mi sandwich an' mi mate fell out."

It war this language problem that made a French au-pair girl called Denise so miserable in Hull. This war apart from t'fact that there's nowt to do i' Hull after 8 o'clock cos it's i'only place ah've ever been where t'taxi drivers ask you where they can get a woman. Any road Denise is crying 'er eyes out one night in't Wellington Club when she bumps into a sailor. Ee sez ee'll take back 'ome to France. Provided she'll sleep in 'is cabin with 'im. She agrees so ee smuggles 'er on board that very night.

T'ships sails next morning, but it's dead rough and t'sailor's no gentleman. Being a real Yorkshireman ee wants value for t'money ee's not spent. Five days later she thinks they must now be in France. Sea sick, battered, bedraggled, Denise staggers on 'tbridge t' t'captain. "Oooo Monsieur, I am sorry I am ze stowaway. Please we must be in France by now."

"France lass," sez the Captain, "France? This is the Hull to Grimsby Ferry."

I were born i' Bratford in't days when t'fowk war white ant' buildings war black. Now things 'ave changed a lot, to give yer a merry jest ah read in t'Enoch Powell Bumper Racialist Fun book. It's not that t'immigrants 'ave made a big difference to most of us though t'traffic wardens 'ave been pretty busy giving parking tickets to t'armoured cars in Lumb Lane since old Bangla Dashed away from Pakistan. But they 'ave given us a whole new series of Yorkshire jokes. Like the one our kid told me about when ee war queueing i' Huddersfield for t'bus to Brighouse after Huddersfield Town 'ad been lossin' at 'ome. Huddersfield Corporation bus comes up. Packed. "Sorry," bawls the Pakistani conductor. "Me ram-jam full." Ant'chap behind our lad bawls out, "Ah don't want to know thi name. Ah just want to get ont'bloody bus."

They've 'ad their problems in Leeds, too. In fact ah war reading in t'*Evening Post* t'other neet that Leeds Corporation war bricking up t'bottom of all t'public conveniences in Chapeltown to stop limbo dancers getting in free. But it's Bradford that 'as most immigrants. In fact so many that a nurse at Bradford Royal Infirmary wor telling me when I went in for me pre-frontal lobotomy that when they'd advertised for donors for Bradford's first heart transplant operation the only one to come forward was a Pakistani, Nawz Jamil Boothroyd, from Peel Terrace in Lumb Lane. Ee war ready to give 'is heart to improve race relations i'Bradford. So they teks 'im off i' great state to meet the patient, or do they call 'im the victim, in the heart transplant operation? There ee is lying in bed wheezing, pale and deathlike, as if ee's stayed up late every neet to watch *Coronation Street.* And when ee seez the Pakistani coming into 'is room ee goes even more pale and death-like. "Good morning," the nurse heard Nawaz Jamil say. "I'm the man who's giving you his heart." "Thank Christ for that," sez the man who's going to get the new heart. "For a minute I thought you'd come to tell me you were buying t'house next door."

Still at least trade i'fowk isn't all one way. Colonel Bagshaw Smyth from Knottingley Manor House actually went out to Pakistan to advise the Pak. Post Office on the introduction of Substandard Trunk Dialling ("Don't do it" ee told 'em). Ee found 'em all very 'ard working and conscientious ee wrote 'ome to tell the Knottingley *Chronicle and Budgerigar Fanciers Gazette*. Except one week when he got to a big town in the interior and found everyone lying around, sunbathing, eating ice cream, doing nowt at all. "What the devil's going on here. Why are you all lazing around?" he bawls in best military fashion. "Well, Sahib," the postmaster explains, "this is Bowling Tide week."

Owereard i' Lumb Lane (East) t'other day. "Would you want your daughter to marry Enoch Powell?" "Course not, ee's already married."

Some seem to think us Yorkshire fowk are mean. My dad's that close ee wudn't tell yer tomorrow war Tuesday if yer didn't ask 'im. But in any case it int, so that dunt matter. I 'ave 'eard of some fowk so mean they wouldn't part wi't'reek of their own muck, but most on us aren't mean. We just chuck us money around like a man wi'no arms. Ow do yer think millowners get to be millowners if it in't by waiting to read t'*Telegraph an' Argus* until it's wrapped round their fish an' chips? In fact, our Auntie Clara once worked for one on't'meanest on 'em. Mr. Craddock, gaffer at Prospect Mill i'Mixendon. Ee war a reet self made man — an' ee worshipped 'is creator an' all, she used to tell me. Still t'time came when ee 'ad to retire from t'business an' part wi' some o't'brass. So ee sets off on a world cruise on a liner that big it made Saltaire Mills look like our pigeon loft. Craddock had ordered the best. Suite on A deck. Air Condimenting. Two Stewards. First day on board t'Purser come up to 'im. "Captain's compliments Mr. Craddock and he's asked me to request the pleasure of the company of yourself and Mrs. Craddock at his table for the duration of the voyage." "Then ee must be daft," says Craddock. "After ah've paid all that good brass for t'tickets tha dunt expect me to eat wi't'crew does tha?"

It's very rare that Yorkshire fowk let money go to their 'eads — or to anyone else's pockets for that matter. Like old Joss Akroyd i'Royston. Saturday neet ee finds out ee's won £400,000 on t'pools. More money than Vivienne Nicholson's spent. Celebrating all day Sunday yet come Monday morning

there ee is int'clocking in queue back at Redfearn's Glassworks. "Nay, Joss, tha's not going to carry on working nah that tha's won 400,000 quid are yer?"
"Not I, me old love," sez Joss, "ah've cum back for me pot."

Still that's not as mean as a lad ah was at school wi' at Woodbottom Council School. 'Is name war Keith Jagger an' ah suppose ee cudn't 'elp it. All t'family war that way inclined. Any road ee's living i' Baildon an' ee's tekin out this lass from Riddlesden about ten miles away so they meet in Bingley. If ee meets 'er outside t'Myrtle cinema ee might 'ave to pay for 'er so he arranges to get there first and go in by 'imself, reckoning that ee's saving 'er a seat. When they come out ee let's 'er pay for 'is fish and chips across in't Myrtle Fish Bar. Then ee won't tek 'er 'ome cos it'll cost too much to go there 'an back on't' bus. All he'll do is to give 'er a tanner for 'er fare. So off she goes on t'Keighley West Yorkshire bus, tramps up 'ome and bursts inter tears telling 'er mother all about 'ow mean Keith Jagger's been. "Well, ah nivver 'eard nowt like it," sez her mother, "the skinny devil. Ere's a tanner for 'im an' two bob for thee. Get t'bus and tek 'im back 'is tanner this minute." So the lass goes back down to the bus changes at t'Branch, gets a Baildon bus and marches up to Jagger's door on Woodbottom. Young Keith comes to t'door. "Ello luv. Forgotten summat?" "Nay, me mam sez to give yer yer tanner back. An 'ere it is," an with that she chucks it at 'im. "Nay," sez Keith, picking it up, "tha shouldn't'a bothered. It'd a done int'morning."

Young Barry used to run to school down a snicket past Charlton's Farm every morning. And every day he would make young Charlton furious by yelling as he ran:

"Hey — oo puts watter in t'milk?"

After a week or two of this young Charlton gets right sick and went to see the Headmaster at Barry's school. So Barry was given a real ticking-off and threatened with the cane if he shouted those words at young Charlton again.

Next morning there was the clatter of Barry's clogs in the snicket. Young Charlton looked up from the milking and grinned. Then he heard Barry's voice.

"Hey," shouted Barry.

"What's up now?" demand young Charlton.

"Tha knows!" yelled back Barry.

Herbert was feeling right lonely. So he went into the middle of town to a pet shop. There in the window was a lovely pup — a black Cocker Spaniel — little, daft, with eyes like a baby. In goes Herbert and buys him for a fiver. Out he came proud as a new dad.

"Tha's a reet beauty," said Herbert, as the pup licked his face, "even tho' tha's good for nowt."

So Herbert took the pup for a walk by the canal. Casually he threw a stick across the water and next thing he knows the pup is after it. Only thing is the pup isn't doing the bog-paddle, he's actually TROTTING ACROSS THE SURFACE OF THE WATER.

Back comes the pup with the stick and Herbert picks him up. The pup's feet are bone dry.

"Ah've got a reet bargain 'ere," said Herbert.

So he ran to his mate Charlie's house and dragged him down to the canal bank.

"Nah then," says Herbert, "just thee watch this."

Herbert hurled the stick away across the water. Off goes the pup, toddles over the water and comes back with the stick — bone-dry.

Herbert was fair flummoxed at Charlie's reaction. His pal was howling with laughter.

"Ere," says Herbert, "ere Cleverclogs, shut up laughin' and admit me pup's a ruddy marvel . . . ee's a reet bargain for a fiver."

"Bargain," spluttered Charlie, "bargain! 'Appen tha's been done 'Erbert. Bloody mutt can't even swim."

By now you should know what sort of man is a Yorkshireman. But there's still some rum uns. Like t'bloke standing on top o't Merrion Centre i' Leeds threatening to commit suicide. "My wife's left me. I don't know what to do. I'm going to end it all," ee yells. There's a bloke from Heckmondwike int'crowd an' ee decides to use good Yorkshire common sense. So he shouts up t'bloke, "Don't do a daft thing like that. Think about yer Yorkshire Pudding on Sunday."

No effect. "I'm going to jump."

T'Heckmondwike bloke decides to make 'im laugh. Tells 'im a funny Yorkshire story about someone dying.

No effect. "I'm going to jump."

"Think about t'lovely country. Think ont'Dales. Think on Ilka Moor."

"I'm going to jump."

"Well think about our Freddy."

"Freddy? Freddy who?"

"Jump yer beggar. Jump."